Nature's Cycles

The Rock Cycle

Sally Morgan

PowerKiDS press.

New York

Published in 2009 by The Rosen Publishing Group Inc.
29 East 21st Street, New York, NY 10010

First Edition

Series editor: Nicola Edwards
Designer: Jason Billin

Library of Congress Cataloging-in-Publication Data

Morgan, Sally.
   The rock cycle / Sally Morgan. — 1st ed.
      p. cm. — (Nature's cycles)
   Includes index.
   ISBN 978-1-4358-2865-0 (library binding)
   ISBN 978-1-4358-2947-3 (paperback)
   ISBN 978-1-4358-2951-0 (6-pack)
   1. Petrology—Juvenile literature. 2. Geochemical cycles—Juvenile literature.
   I. Title.
   QE432.2.M662 2009
   552—dc22

                         2008025733

Manufactured in China

Picture acknowledgments: Cover: Main image Genevieve Leaper/Ecoscene; stones
Anthony Cooper/Ecoscene; tor Andrew Brown/Ecoscene; lava Robert Nichol/
Ecoscene

Title page Genevieve Leaper/Ecoscene; p4 Andrew Brown/ Ecoscene; p5, p6 Andrew
Brown/ Ecoscene; p7t John Farmar/ Ecoscene, p7b. Anthony Cooper/ Ecoscene;
p8t Erik Schaffer/ Ecoscene, p8b Kevin King/ Ecoscene; p9 top clock Chinch
Gryniewicz/ Ecoscene, Angela Hampton/ Ecoscene,.Sally Morgan/ Ecoscene,
Chinch Gryniewicz/ Ecoscene; p11t Andrew Brown/ Ecoscene; p11b Erik
Schaffer/ Ecoscene; p12 Robert Nichol/ Ecoscene - also on contents;
 p13t Wayne Lawler/ Ecoscene; p13b Quentin Bates/ Ecoscene;
p14 Ecoscene - Papilio /Robert Pickett; p15 Nick Hawkes/
Ecoscene; p16 Genevieve Leaper/ Ecoscene; p17 Paul Thompson/
Ecoscene; p18t Sally Morgan/ Ecoscene; p18b. Martin Jones/
Ecoscene; p19 Fritz Polking/ Ecoscene; p20 Andrew Brown/
Ecoscene; p21t Fritz Polking/ Ecoscene; p21b. Peter McGrath/
Ecoscene; p22, p23 (both) John Farmar/ Ecoscene; p24 Chris
Chelmick/ Ecoscene; p25, p26 Peter Hulme/ Ecoscene;
p27t Sally Morgan/ Ecoscene; p27, p28 Nick Hawkes/
Ecoscene; p29 Judyth Platt/ Ecoscene

Artwork by Ian Thompson

Contents

What is a rock?   4

Rocks beneath our feet   6

Rock types   8

Igneous rocks   10

Volcanic rocks   12

Sedimentary rocks   14

Changing rocks   16

Worn away   18

Weathered shapes   20

Washed up   22

Soil   24

Types of soil   26

Rocks and pollution   28

Glossary   30

Further Information and Web Sites   31

Index   32

What is a rock?

Rocks are everywhere, in the ground beneath our feet and in backyards and parks. They form mountains and cliffs. Some are used to build structures and others are so attractive that they are made into jewelry.

Inside a rock

A rock is made of minerals. Minerals are natural substances that occur in the ground. They are neither animal nor plant, but substances such as salt, metal, or sulfur. Coal is a mineral made of carbon, and the mineral quartz contains almost pure silica. Rocks differ in the minerals that they contain and each rock has its own distinctive mix of minerals.

Rocks usually occur as large masses. Natural processes break rocks down into smaller fragments, which we call stones and pebbles. Even smaller fragments of rock form sand, silt, and clay.

○ Water is an important part of the rock cycle since running water wears away rocks.

In Focus: Rock as a habitat

Rocks provide important habitats for plants and animals. There are lots of cracks running through a mass of rock. Water and soil collect in these cracks. Large cracks on the surface of a rock are perfect places for small plants, such as mosses and ferns, to grow. However, there is too little soil for larger plants. Animals such as wood lice and spiders are found in the cracks, too, sheltering from the sun and wind. Birds nest on ledges on a rock face.

△ Many mountain ranges are formed from granite rock, such as this one in the French Alps.

Ancient rocks

Most rocks are millions of years old. Many were formed before the dinosaurs existed. We know this because, embedded in rocks, scientists have found the fossil remains of strange animals that lived in the oceans hundreds of millions of years ago.

Investigate: Carbon

Carbon is a very common element that is found in the ground. It occurs in several forms, such as diamonds, graphite, coal, and charcoal. Use the Internet to find out more about the different forms of carbon and the uses to which they can be put.

The rock cycle

The rock cycle begins with the formation of the rocks. Some are formed quickly in just a few weeks, but others are formed very slowly, over millions of years. Many rocks are hidden beneath the Earth's surface. The rocks that lie on the surface are exposed to wind and water, and they get worn away, or eroded. Fragments of rock, such as pebbles and sand, are carried away and end up in rivers and then the sea. There, these particles of rocks eventually form new rocks.

Rocks beneath our feet

Rock is found underneath every surface. If you dig a hole in the ground, you eventually come to a layer of hard rock beneath the soil. In most places, the rock is covered by soil. However, where the rock is not covered, it forms features such as cliffs and mountain tops.

▼ This traditional alpine house in Switzerland is made from local stone.

Rocks for building

Most rocks are hard and have many uses. They are ideal building materials, because they are hard-wearing and most are impermeable. This means that water runs off them rather than through them. Rocks can be used to make the walls of buildings to keep out the rain, wind, and sun. They are used as a flooring material, too. For example, sandstone is cut into thin layers called flagstones and laid over the floor. In many hot countries such as Morocco and Spain, homes have smooth marble floors that are cool in the summer.

Investigate: Rocks in the home

How many different types of rock can you find in your home? Have a look at the walls: are they made from stone or brick? Remember that concrete contains sand and gravel. There may be decorative items made of rocks, such as granite and marble, or jewelry with precious stones. Feel each rock that you find. Is it smooth, rough, hard, or soft?

Sand and gravel

Sand and gravel are two essential materials used by the building industry. The only difference between sand and gravel is the size of the rock particles. Sand is made up of small grains of rock, and gravel is formed from larger particles such as pebbles. Sand and gravel have many uses, such as making paths and children's sandboxes, and they are essential for making concrete. Concrete is an important building material. To make concrete, sand and gravel are mixed with cement and water. The runny mix hardens to form a solid, stonelike material.

In Focus: Precious gemstones

Diamonds, emeralds, and rubies are just three examples of precious stones. The minerals that make up precious gemstones give color and catch the light. This makes the stones attractive and valuable. Often, the gemstone that is dug straight from the ground looks nothing like the stone that is used in jewelry. The raw stones have to be cleaned, cut, and polished to produce the final stone.

⊙ A quarry is a place where rock is dug out of the ground.

▶ Diamonds, opals, and emeralds have been used in these pieces of jewelry.

Rock types

There are many different types of rock and they are grouped according to how they were formed and the mix of minerals that they contain.

Minerals

There are more than 3,000 different minerals in existence, but only about 30 are found in rocks. Some rocks contain several minerals, but other rocks are made from just one or two different minerals. If you looked closely at a piece of granite rock with a magnifying glass, you would see that it is made up of several different minerals, including mica, quartz, and feldspar. Each mineral is of a slightly different color and size, and they are all stuck together.

Rock properties

Rocks vary in their hardness and ability to take up water. A piece of chalk, for example, is quite soft and you can scrape the surface with a fingernail. In contrast, diamond is one of the hardest substances, so hard that it is used in many industries to cut through metal and stone. Diamond powder is used as an abrasive to produce a smooth surface. Rocks such as basalt are incredibly heavy, but pumice is full of air so it is incredibly light. Some rocks are porous. This means that the spaces between the minerals can become filled with water. Chalk is a porous rock.

Permeable rocks allow water to flow through them. Chalk, limestone, and sandstone are permeable rocks. This limits their usefulness. For example, limestone and chalk are not used for kitchen counters, because they take up liquids and stain easily. Most rocks, such as slate, are impermeable. Slate is used to make roof tiles, because it keeps water out.

⬆ Quartz is formed of silicon dioxide and is the most common mineral on Earth.

⬇ This home is close to a crumbling cliff and soon it will fall into the sea.

Forming rocks

Although there are many types of rock, they are formed in just one of three ways. Igneous rocks are formed when molten (liquid) magma from deep in the Earth cools and becomes solid. Sedimentary rocks form over millions of years from layers of sediment. Metamorphic rocks are igneous or sedimentary rocks that have been altered in some way by natural processes. The following pages will explore how the different types of rocks are formed and how they differ from each other.

Investigate: Rock features

Collect some samples of different rocks, such as chalk, slate, granite, and marble. First, test how hard each is by scratching the surface with a sharp object. Can you see a mark on the rock surface? Now see if each is porous by carefully dripping one drop of water on the surface of the rock. Does the water disappear? Can you think of a use for a porous rock?

The Rock Cycle

Rocks are broken into smaller pieces by water and ice.

Water wears away the rock and carries small particles to the sea.

Layers of sand build up on the sea floor and in time form rock. When the land is uplifted, the rock may appear above ground.

Igneous rocks

Deep inside the Earth, it is so hot that the rock is liquid. Liquid rock is called magma. Magma is less dense than the rock lying above it, so it flows up through cracks toward the surface.

Crystals

As magma moves toward the surface, it cools. In some places, the magma explodes out of cracks as lava. In other places, the magma is trapped in pockets in the ground. As the magma cools, crystals appear. The crystallization process continues until all the magma is solid and has formed an igneous rock.

Igneous rocks vary in the size of their crystals. If the magma cools quickly, for example, if magma pours into the cold water of an ocean, the crystals are small, but magma that cools slowly in the ground has larger crystals of more than 0.75 inch (20 millimeters) across.

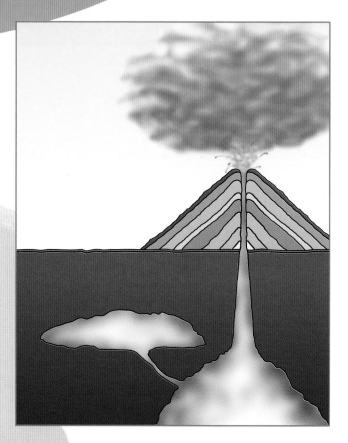

⬤ Some magma is forced up to the surface and pours out of the ground as lava. Over time, layers of lava build up and form a volcano. Some magma remains trapped underground where it cools and forms rock.

In Focus: Inside the Earth

The uppermost layer in the Earth is called the crust. It is up to 56 miles (90 kilometers) thick under the continents and about 3.7 miles (6 km) thick under the oceans. About 95 percent of the Earth's crust is made up of igneous rock. Beneath the crust is the mantle, a layer that is 1,864 miles (3000 km) thick. The magma in the mantle is very thick and slow-moving, a little bit like molasses.

Intrusive rocks

Igneous rocks that form deep in the ground are called intrusive igneous rocks. They are ancient rocks that have cooled and solidified over millions of years. Most intrusive igneous rocks remain hidden, often under a layer of sedimentary rock. However, movements in the Earth's crust can cause the igneous rocks to be thrust upward. When the overlying rocks are worn away by wind and water, the igneous rocks are exposed.

Granites, gabbros, and kimberlites are examples of intrusive igneous rocks. The four main minerals in granite are feldspar, quartz, biotite, and muscovite. Gabbro contains large crystals, more than 0.04 in. (1 mm) in size. This dark, often greenish rock is rich in minerals, such as chromium, nickel, cobalt, gold, silver, and platinum. Intrusive igneous rocks are often rich in precious gemstones, such as diamonds, topaz, and emerald. For example, diamonds are found in kimberlite.

⚠ The Cheesewring in Cornwall, U.K., is a pile of granite rocks known as a tor. The surrounding softer rock has been eroded, leaving just the granite.

⚠ If you look at a piece of granite through a magnifying glass, you will see it is made up of many different minerals.

Investigate: Granite

Granite is used in kitchens and bathrooms as a decorative and hard-wearing rock for work surfaces. There are up to 100 different types of granite, each differing in its mineral content. The colors range from virtually pink to jet black. Use the Internet to search for websites that sell granite. Look at the photographs of the different colors of granite that are available. See if you can find out how the minerals in a black granite differ from those in a pink granite.

Volcanic rocks

Volcanic eruptions are impressive but frightening natural events. The lava that escapes from a volcano is magma that has reached the surface. The lava may explode from the volcano or flow out of cracks. Rivers of lava run down the sides of the volcano.

From lava to rock

When the lava cools, it forms extrusive igneous rock or volcanic rock. Usually the lava cools slowly over weeks or even months. Sometimes the lava cools in just a few days, and there is no time for the minerals in the lava to form crystals. When this happens, the lava forms a type of volcanic glass called obsidian.

Obsidian is a very dense rock that does not allow light to pass through it. This means it looks almost black. However, a tiny sliver of obsidian is transparent, because the light can pass straight through it.

◀ Red hot lava flows from a Hawaiian volcano into the sea.

The fertile soils around this volcano in Indonesia are used to grow rice.

When lava cools slowly, small crystals form. The most common volcanic rock is basalt, which has crystals so small that they cannot be seen with the eye alone. Basalt forms from dark, thick lava that is rich in iron and magnesium. The black sand on some Hawaiian beaches comes from weathered basalt. Pumice is another volcanic rock that has tiny crystals. It is a pale rock that is very light in weight, because it is full of tiny holes. The holes were left when the volcanic gases bubbled out.

In Focus: Volcanoes and lava

The lava that forms volcanoes is weathered by the wind and rain. The lava breaks up and soil starts to form. In time, the slopes of volcanoes such as Mount Teide in Tenerife and Mount Etna in Sicily, Italy, become covered in soils that are used to grow crops and vines. However, these two volcanoes are still active and are likely to produce new lava that would be a threat to the people living close by.

Investigate: Pumice

Pumice has many uses in cosmetics. Pumice stones can be bought as exfoliants to rub dry skin off the soles of feet. It is also used in toothpaste and hand cleaners. You can buy pumice stones from drug stores. Look closely to see the tiny holes in the pumice. Will the stone float in water? Soak your feet in water and then see if you can remove rough skin with the pumice.

The hexagonal columns forming this cliff in Iceland are made from basalt.

Sedimentary rocks

Sedimentary rocks cover about three-quarters of the world's surface. The most common sedimentary rock is shale. This rock makes up half of all sedimentary rocks. About 30 percent of sedimentary rocks are sandstones, and 20 percent are limestones. Sedimentary rocks are made up of many tiny particles of rock that are stuck together.

⊙ If you break open a piece of limestone, you may be lucky enough to find a fossil.

Layers of rock

Sedimentary rocks form under large bodies of water over millions of years. The first stage in the formation of a sedimentary rock is the building up of a layer of sediment on the bottom of lakes and seas. The sediment contains sand, silt, and clay, which have come from rocks. The remains of dead plants and animals drop to the sea or lake bed, too, and add to the sediment.

In Focus: Fossils

When marine animals become fossilized, the soft parts of their bodies break down, but the hard parts, such as the shells, remain. A fossil is an exact copy of the original animal except that it is hard and rocklike. Common fossils in limestone are ammonites and trilobites, animals that were common in the oceans 300 million years ago.

From sediment to rock

As more sediment collects, the lower layers are squashed by the weight of all the overlying layers. In time, thick layers of sediment build up. The sediments become rocks when all the particles are stuck together. The "glue" comes from the various minerals in the sediment. For example, sandstone contains grains of quartz that are glued together with silica and calcite.

Investigate: Layered rocks

In this investigation, you will make sedimentary rock. Take a half-gallon plastic bottle, sand, four different food colorings, and some spackle. Wear a pair of plastic gloves to mix one of the food colors into some sand and spackle, and pour it into the bottom of the plastic bottle. Add more layers, each time using a different color, until you reach the top of the bottle. Allow it to harden for a few days, then cut off the plastic bottle to reveal the layers of sedimentary rocks.

Layers of sedimentary rock can be seen clearly on this cliff in southern England.

Changing rocks

Rocks can be changed by forces, such as the heat from a volcano, or from the pressures exerted when two sections of the Earth's crust push against each other. The rocks are altered so much that they turn into a new type of rock. These rocks are metamorphic, or changed, rocks.

Moving plates

The Earth's crust is a thin layer that floats on the magma in the mantle. The crust is broken into large pieces called plates. As the magma moves around, it causes the plates to move, too. When two plates collide with each other, the crust is pushed up and mountains are formed. For example, the Himalayas have been formed by the Indian plate moving north and pushing against the Asian plate, causing the crust in between to crumple and push up to form a mountain range. This has happened very slowly, over millions of years. The process is still continuing, since the Himalayas are becoming taller by a few inches every year.

⬤ The highest mountain peak in the world is Everest in the Himalayas. Mount Everest, which is to the left of the center of this photograph, is 29,028 ft. (8,848 m) high.

The effects of change

When rocks are changed by pressure or heat, they often become tougher and more crystalline. For example, heat changes sandstone to a hard metaquartzite, and intense pressure changes limestone into marble. Rocks that are changed by pressure are crushed, and they take on a banded or layered appearance. Pressure changes mudstone and shale into slate. If there is even more pressure, mudstone becomes a type of rock called gneiss. It has a banded appearance with layers of different minerals. The pressure can cause fossils in the rock to be distorted or twisted.

In Focus: Earthquakes

Earthquakes are caused by the Earth's plates moving past each other. During an earthquake, the ground shakes, buildings collapse, and large cracks appear in the ground. Most of the world's earthquakes occur around the edge of the Pacific plate, affecting Southeast Asia, Australia, Japan, Canada, the United States, and South America. The fourth most powerful earthquake since 1900 occurred under the Indian Ocean in 2004. It caused the tsunami that killed over 200,000 people in Indonesia, Thailand, and Sri Lanka. In 2005, powerful earthquakes rocked the Himalayas and the island of Sumatra in Indonesia.

Investigate: Marble

Marble is a very popular building material, because it is hard and can be polished to give a smooth, shiny surface. Its name comes from the Greek word meaning "shining stone." Many places or structures have marble in their name, for example, Marble Arch in London, U.K. Can you find examples of places or structures that have marble in their name and some pictures of buildings that are built from marble?

⬇ One of the most famous buildings in the world is the Taj Mahal in Agra, India. It was built from white marble from Rajasthan.

17

Worn away

The next stage in the rock cycle occurs when rocks are exposed to sun, wind, and rain and they are worn away. This is called weathering or erosion. Some rocks are weathered more easily, for example, chalk, but others, such as granite, are tough and resistant to weather.

Flowing water

Water running over a rock slowly wears it away. This is because the water carries particles, such as grains of sand, that rub the surface. The rocks at the bottom of a stream have been worn smooth by flowing water. Over millions of years, the power of fast-flowing water along a river erodes any rock along the sides and the bottom, creating banks and even deep gorges.

⬤ The Grand Canyon is one of the world's deepest gorges, and it has been formed by the River Colorado. Layers of different sedimentary rock are exposed on the sides of the gorge.

Investigate: Weathering

Different types of rock weather at different rates. Rain water is very slightly acidic and the acids in water react with the calcium carbonate in limestone, leaving a rough, pitted surface. Granites are more hard-wearing. Look at the different gravestones in an old cemetery. The dates on the gravestones will tell you how old they are. Find some gravestones of the same age but made from different rock, such as marble, granite, and limestone. Which ones are more weathered? Look for discoloring, pitted surfaces, and crumbling edges.

Shattering rocks

Water can break up huge blocks of rock, too. Water seeps through cracks in rock. When temperatures fall to freezing, any water in the cracks turns to ice. When water freezes, it expands, so the ice pushes on the surrounding rock and opens up the crack. When the ice melts, the rock shatters. This process is called freeze-thaw.

Mountain slopes are often covered by rock fields made up of lots of small broken rocks. These rock fields are created by freeze-thaw in the rock cliffs. The bits of rock break off and tumble down onto the slope below. These slopes are very unstable and only the most nimble of animals, such as mountain goats, can cross them.

Wind action

Wind can erode rocks, too. This is because wind picks up tiny particles from the ground and rubs them against rocks. Over time, the rocks are worn away. Desert rocks often have a shiny surface called desert varnish, which is created by the erosion. Also, wind erosion can create grooves and depressions in the rock that get larger over time, creating interesting rock shapes.

⚫ The action of water over thousands of years has eroded the rock in this part of Utah, leaving white limestone spires that look like giant toadstools.

In Focus: Sandblasting

Stone that has become dirty with grime can be cleaned using a method called sandblasting. This mimics the natural process of wind erosion by directing a jet of sand at the surface of the stone. The particles of sand wear away the dirty top layer, revealing a clean surface underneath.

Weathered shapes

The weathering of rocks by wind and water has created some of the world's best known landscapes. The National Parks of North America are home to amazing natural arches, canyons, and weird rock shapes that attract millions of visitors each year. Weathering takes place underground, too, creating caves.

Rock arches

Arches National Park in Utah has more than 2,000 sandstone arches. Over millions of years, water has seeped through the soft sandstone rocks, opening up cracks and causing huge boulders to drop off. Wind has blown away all the fine particles and this has smoothed the surface of the rock. Over time, this has created the arches. There are single and double arches, windows and columns. The erosion is still continuing and since 1970, almost 50 arches have collapsed.

◀ Delicate Arch is the most famous arch in Arches National Park. There was an idea to protect the arch by coating it in plastic to protect it from erosion. However, the suggestion was thought to be impractical and was not put into practice.

In Focus: Rock landscapes and tourism

Millions of people visit the rock landscapes of Grand Canyon National Park in Arizona, and Arches National Park and Bryce Canyon in Utah. However, there has to be a balance between conserving the landscape and allowing people to enjoy it. As people walk over the rocks, their feet erode the surface, just like water and wind. Climbing can dislodge rocks, damage arches, and open up more cracks to water. In the National Parks, the areas over which people can roam are restricted to certain paths, so the landscape is protected.

⬥ This narrow canyon in Arizona has been carved by wind and rain, leaving behind a wonderful corkscrewlike surface to the sandstone rock.

Forming caves

Most caves form in soft rock such as limestone. Water seeping down through cracks dissolves the surface of the limestone, making the cracks larger. When the crack is large enough, water can flow through the rock. The cracks become larger still and an underground stream forms. As more rock is worn away, a network of caves, underground passages, and streams is formed.

Investigate: Conserving buildings

Next time you visit an ancient monument or historic building, look at the features that are made from stone, such as steps, floors, and walls. Notice how the rubbing of feet over hundreds of years has made stone steps and floors shiny. Are there signs of the stone being worn away? Look at the edges of stone walls near entrances. The action of hundreds of people rubbing past gradually wears away the stone. Look for ways in which the structure of the building is protected, for example, by the placing clear sheets of Perspex over stone walls so they are protected but can still be seen.

Washed up

The particles that are created by weathering have an important role to play in the rock cycle. They are blown away by the wind or carried by water and end up in rivers and the sea. The particles build up layers of sediment that, in time, turn into sedimentary rock.

Meandering rivers

A fast-flowing stream tumbling down a mountainside picks up particles that are carried downstream. Some rivers carry so many particles that their waters are murky. For example, the Huang Ho River in China is also called the Yellow River, because it carries so much silt.

As a river gets closer to the sea, the water flows more slowly. It may meander, or form snakelike loops, across the land. When water flows around a bend in the river, the flow is fastest on the outside of the bend and slowest on the inside. Sediment is dropped on the inside bend and this builds up to form sand banks. Even more sediment is dropped when the river reaches the sea. The sediment builds up to form a muddy estuary.

⬥ This river is meandering across a valley as it nears the sea.

In Focus: The importance of mud

When a river reaches the sea, the sediment is dropped. Over time, the sediment builds up into banks of sticky mud called mudflats. At low tide, the mudflats are exposed. Mud is important for wildlife, since it is full of nutrients. Marine animals, such as lugworms and cockles, live in the mud. They are then fed upon by wading birds, such as dunlin, shelduck, and knot. There are seals and turtles and plenty of fish, too. Flatfish, such as plaice and sole hide, under the surface of the sediment and catch small animals.

Changing coastlines

Rocks that form coastlines are under constant attack from the waves. Harder rocks erode more slowly and they form headlands that stick out from the coast as softer rocks are worn away, and this creates an indentation on the coast called a bay.

All the eroded particles of rock are carried by the tides into the bays to form beaches. The sand on a beach is always moving. When waves hit a coastline at an angle, the sand is carried along the coast. In some places, the sand builds up to form new beaches, but on other parts of the coast, sand may be carried away.

△ Lulworth Cove in England was formed by the sea eroding the softer rock to form the bay, leaving the harder rock as headlands.

Investigate: Pebbly beaches

Pebbles on a beach are moved around by the waves and they are gradually sorted out by their size. The larger pebbles are moved higher up the beach than the smaller ones. Next time you visit a pebbly beach, look closely at the pebbles. Start at the water's edge and measure the diameter of 10 pebbles. Measure another 10 pebbles on the middle of the beach and then 10 from the top of the beach. Work out the average diameter of the 10 pebbles (add up the 10 values and divide by 10). Does the size change from the top to the bottom?

▽ The pebbles on this beach have been sorted according to their size by the water.

Soil

Weathering is an important part of the rock cycle. Many of the weathered particles of rock end up in water and form new sedimentary rocks. However, weathering can also lead to the formation of soil.

Soil formation

When rocks are exposed to the weather, they crumble and become covered with a layer of rock fragments. Plants start to grow among the fragments. Dead leaves get mixed in, too. Over thousands, even millions of years, the soil becomes thicker. The speed with which the soil forms depends on many factors. These include the type of rock, the climate, how much plant and animal activity is taking place, and whether the soil is on the level or on a slope.

In Focus: Soil organisms

Up to one billion bacteria may be found in just 0.035 ounce (one gram) of soil. There are larger animals, too, such as threadlike nematode worms, ants, beetle larvae, and most importantly, earthworms. Earthworms burrow through the soil and are important for mixing the organic matter into the soil and creating air spaces and helping drainage. This improves the soil for plants.

◀ This alpine plant is growing between the rocks, trapping water and leaves. In time, a thin soil builds up.

Some of the youngest soils are those that are forming on lava and on sand dunes. Among the oldest, which are thousands of years old, are the deep black soils of the prairies of the Midwestern United States.

Sand, silt, and clay

Soil contains three types of particle: sand, silt, and clay, of which clay is the smallest. There is organic matter, too. This is the decayed remains of plants and animals. Soil particles are round in shape, so there are plenty of air spaces and water around them, too.

Soil erosion

Soil may take a long time to form, but it can be washed away in a matter of days. Most soils are covered by plants, which help to protect the soil from the sun, wind, and rain. Plant roots hold the soil particles together. When the plants are removed, the soil is dried by the sun, then blown away by wind. Water washes soil away, especially on slopes.

Investigate: Soil

To see if a soil contains large amounts of sand or clay, try these simple tests. Take a handful of soil. Does it crumble easily in your hand? What is the texture of the soil? Make the soil wet and see if you can shape the soil with your fingers. Now place some soil in a small plastic plant pot with holes in the bottom and add some water. How quickly does the water drain off? A sandy soil is very crumbly, has a gritty texture and drains quickly. A clay soil feels smooth, it will not crumble, and it can be molded into shapes with the fingers. Water drains slowly through a clay soil.

Dry, sandy soil is easily blown away when it is left exposed without any plant cover.

Types of soil

There are many different soils around the world. They vary in depth and color, and in the amount of sand, silt, and clay that they contain.

Soil profiles

Soil is made up of distinct layers. On the top is a layer of dead and decaying matter such as leaf litter. Beneath this layer is the topsoil. The topsoil is dark in color, because it is rich in organic matter. Beneath the topsoil is the subsoil, which is much paler. The layer beneath the subsoil is very stony and below this is the bedrock.

Investigate: Soil profiles

Look at the profile of the soil in your yard or school grounds. Dig a deep hole with a shovel. Make sure you cut vertically down on one side of the hole, so that you can see the layers clearly. Now look at the profile. Can you see the topsoil and the subsoil?

◁ The topsoil beneath the grass is a darker color than the subsoil below.

topsoil

subsoil

Different soils

A podzol is an acid, sandy soil that forms under conifer forests and heathlands. A chernozem is a deep brown or black soil with a good mix of sand, silt, and clay. It forms under grassland on the Prairies of North America and on the Steppes of Russia. Desert soils are very thin and lack organic matter. The heat draws water and salts into the topsoil. The water evaporates, leaving the salts behind on the surface.

Tropical soils

The intense heat and high rainfall in tropical areas causes rocks to be weathered more quickly than in other places. The rain washes away many of the useful minerals, such as potassium, and leaves behind iron and quartz. These minerals form a red soil called a laterite. Some laterites are very hard and can be cut into blocks and used as bricks. In part of Africa, hard laterite soils are used to make road surfaces.

⚫ Red laterite soils, seen here in Kenya, are clay soils with a high iron and aluminum content.

⚫ The dark brown, almost black color of this soil is due to the presence of a lot of organic matter.

In Focus: Soils for farming

The best soils for farming are loams. A loam is a soil that has a good mix of sand, silt, and clay. This means that the water drains through the soil, but not as quickly as in a sandy soil, nor does it get waterlogged like a clay soil. Farming soils have to be rich in organic matter and minerals, so that crop plants such as wheat and corn grow well. Some of the best farming soils are found in the Fens of Britain, on the North American Prairies, and on the Russian Steppes.

Rocks and pollution

The rock cycle can be disrupted by air pollution. Air pollution harms plants and animals, and it damages rocks, too. Exposed rock can be eroded by harmful substances in the air, such as sulfur dioxide. Sedimentary rocks, such as limestone, are the most vulnerable rocks.

City stones

The air in towns and cities is polluted by the exhaust fumes from cars and emissions from power stations and other industries. Car exhausts pump out tiny particles of black soot and this makes the stone walls and statues dirty, giving them a black surface.

▶ The wall of this building in Oxford, U.K., has been cleaned to reveal bright, clean stone.

In Focus: Repairing the damage

It is possible to repair some of the damage caused by air pollution. The grimy black coating that covers rocks can be blasted away using sand or water, to leave a new clean surface. However, this cannot be done too many times, because each time, a layer of rock is removed. When stones or statues have been badly damaged, the only way to repair the damage is to replace the stone, using rock of a similar origin.

Acid rain

Rain is naturally slightly acidic and it erodes rocks such as limestone (see pages 18–19). Acid rain is rain that is more acidic than normal. Pollutants, such as sulfur dioxide and nitrous oxide, rise into the atmosphere and dissolve in water to form weak acids. These acids fall to the ground in rain and wear away the surfaces of rock. Acid rain damages buildings in cities by dissolving the surface of stone, leaving it discolored and pitted. Statues are worn smooth, so that the details on faces and hands are lost.

Around the world, historic buildings are under attack from air pollution. These include the Taj Mahal in India, mosques in North Africa, cathedrals and castles in United Kingdom, and marble monuments in Rome.

⬤ The features on this figurehead on Lincoln Castle in the U.K. can barely be seen, because they have been damaged by pollution.

Investigate: Lichens and air pollution

Lichens are organisms that are part plant and part fungus. There are many different types of lichen. There are encrusting lichens that are gray, yellow, and orange in color. Foliose lichens look like leaves. Others look like small balls of wool. Look at the buildings and trees where you live. The encrusting lichens can grow in polluted places, but the foliose lichens are very sensitive to air pollution. If you find any of the foliose lichens, this means that the air is clean.

Glossary

abrasive A type of substance that is used to rub and grind another material to create a smooth surface.

acid rain Rain that is more acidic than normal due to the presence of weak acids.

bedrock The stony layer of soil beneath the subsoil.

cemented Stuck together, glued.

chernozem A deep, dark brown-black soil that forms under grassland.

concrete A building material made of sand, gravel, cement, and water that is mixed together. It hardens and becomes stonelike.

crystallization The process of forming crystals.

desert varnish The shiny surface on desert rocks that is created by erosion.

element A pure substance, such as carbon, that cannot be separated into any other substances.

erosion The wearing away of rock by wind and water.

estuary The place where a river empties into the sea.

exhaust Waste gases that are pumped out by cars engines and the chimneys of power stations and factories.

extrusive igneous rocks Rocks that form on the surface when lava cools and becomes solid.

fossil The remains of an animal or plant that are preserved in a rock.

freeze-thaw The action of freezing and then melting of water in rock.

gorge A narrow, steep-sided valley with cliffs.

igneous rocks Rocks that are formed from magma. Granites and kimberlites are igneous rocks.

impermeable Not allowing water or other liquids to pass through. Slate is an impermeable rock.

intrusive igneous rocks Rocks that form in the ground when magma cools and becomes solid.

lava The molten (liquid) rocks that comes out of volcanoes. Magma is called lava when it reaches the surface.

lichens Organisms that are formed from an alga (a type of plant) and a fungus.

loam A soil that has a good mix of sand, silt, and clay.

magma Molten or liquid rock beneath the Earth's surface.

meander To wind or bend.

metamorphic rocks Rocks that have undergone change, caused by intense heat or pressure. Marble is a metamorphic rock.

mineral A natural, inorganic substance.

permeable Allowing water or other liquids to pass through. Limestone is a permeable rock

podzol An acidic soil that forms under heathland or conifer forests.

porous Having small pores or holes that allow water to seep through. Chalk is a porous rock.

quarry A large hole in the ground from which rocks are dug.

saturated Completely filled with water.

sediment Particles of sand, silt, and clay that are carried by water and which settle on the bed of a lake, river, or sea.

sedimentary rocks Rocks that are formed from layers of sediment. Shale is a sedimentary rock.

subsoil A lower layer of soil that has less organic matter than topsoil and lies above rock.

topsoil The uppermost layer of soil that is rich in organic matter.

tsunami A huge wave that is formed by an underwater earthquake.

volcano A crack in the Earth's crust through which lava escapes, forming a mountainlike structure. Shield volcanoes have a low shape, and conical volcanoes are taller with steep sides.

weathering The wearing away or breaking down of rocks.

Further Information

Books

DK Eyewitness Books: Rocks and
  Minerals
by R. F. Symes
(DK Children, 2004)

Geology Rocks!: Soil
by Rebecca Faulkner
(Raintree, 2008)

My First Field Guide: Looking at Rocks
by Jennifer Dussling
(Grosset and Dunlop, 2001)

Web Sites

Due to the changing nature of Internet links, PowerKids Press has developed an online list of Web sites related to the subject of this book. This site is updated regularly. Please use this link to access this list: www.powerkidslinks.com/natc/rock

Index

Numbers in **bold** refer to pictures.

acid rain 29, **29**, 30
air pollution 28, 29
animals 4, 5, 14, 19, 22, 24, 25, 28
arches 20, **20**, 21

banks 18, 22
basalt 8, 13
bays 23, **23**
beaches 13, 23, **23**
bedrock 26, 30
building materials 6, **6**, 7

canyons **18**, 20
caves 20, 21, **21**
chalk 8, 9, 14, 18
chernozem 27, 30
cliffs 4, 6, 8, **8**, **15**, 19, 30
climate 24
coastlines 23, **23**
conservation 21, 28
continents 10
crystallization 10, 30

Earth's crust 10, 11, 16, 31
earthquakes 17
erosion 18, 19, **19**, 20, 25, **25**, 30
estuary 22, 30

fossils 5, 14, **14**, 30
freeze-thaw 19, 30

gabbro 11
gemstones 7, 11
gorges 18
Grand Canyon 18, **18**, 21
granite 5, 6, 8, 9, 11, **11**, 18
gravel 6, 7, 30
gravestones 18

habitats 4
headlands 23

igneous rocks 3, 9, 10, 11, 30
impermeable rocks 6, 8, 30

jewelry 4, 6, 7, **7**

kimberlite 11

laterites 27, **27**
lava 10, 12, **12**, 13, 25, 30, 31
lichens 29, 30
limestone 8, 14, 17, 18, 19, 21, 28, 29
loams 27

magma 9, 10, 12, 16, 30
marble 6, 9, 17, **17**, 18, 29
metamorphic rocks 9, 16, 30
minerals 4, 7, 8, 11, 12, 15, 17, 27, 31
mountains 4, **5**, 16, **16**

National Parks 20, 21

obsidian 12
oceans 5, 10, 14

plants 4, 14, 24, **24**, 25, 27, 28, 31

podzol 27, 30
porous rocks 8, 9, 31
pumice 8, 13, **13**

quarry **7**, 31

rivers 5, 12, 22, **22**

sand 4, 5, 6, 7, 13, 14, 15, 18, 19, 22, 23, 25, 26, 27, 28, 30, 31
sandblasting 19
sandstone 6, 8, 15, 17, 20, 21
sediment 9, 14, 15, 22, 31
sedimentary rocks 3, 9, 14, 15, **15**, 24, 28, 31
shale 14, 17
slate 8, 9, 17
soil 3, 4, 6, 12, 13, 24, 25, 26, 27, **27**, 30, 31
soil formation 24
soil profiles 26, **26**
structures 4, 17
subsoil 26, **26**, 30, 31

topsoil 26, **26**, 27, 31

volcanoes 12, 13, **13**, 30, 31

water 4, **4**, 5, 6, 7, 8, 9, **9**, 10, 11, 13, 14, 18, 19, 20, 21, 22, 23, 24, 25, 27, 28, 29, 30, 31
waves 23
weathering 18, 20, 22, 24, 31
wind 4, 5, 6, 11, 12, 13, 18, 19, 20, 21, 22, 25, **25**, 30